Traverse Theatre Company

Unfaithful

by Owen McCafferty

First performed at the Traverse Theatre
3 August 2014

A Traverse Theatre Company Commission

Unfaithful

Owen McCafferty

Company

Tom	**Benny Young**
Joan	**Cara Kelly**
Tara	**Amiera Darwish**
Peter	**Owen Whitelaw**
Director	**Rachel O'Riordan**
Designer	**Gary McCann**
Lighting Designer	**Kevin Treacy**
Composer/Sound Designer	**Debra Salem**
Assistant Director	**Rob Jones**
Production Manager	**Kevin McCallum**
Company Stage Manager	**Gemma Turner**
Deputy Stage Manager	**Charlotte Unwin**
Assistant Stage Manager	**Carrie Taylor**
Assistant Stage Manager	**Izzy Taylor**
Costume Supervisor	**Kat Smith**

Traverse Theatre

New Writing | New Work | International | Festivals | Engagement

Artistic Director **Orla O'Loughlin**
Executive Producer **Linda Crooks**

The epicentre of new writing
(The Independent)

From its conception in 1963, the Traverse has remained a pivotal arts venue in Scotland. Founded to keep the spirit of the Edinburgh festivals alive year-round, the Traverse has an unrivalled national and international reputation as a producer and presenter of new work, staging daring new plays and nurturing new talent. The Traverse is a writer's theatre, having launched the careers of Scotland's most celebrated writers – John Byrne, David Greig, David Harrower, Liz Lochhead and Zinnie Harris. The company is committed to finding the next generation of Scottish playwriting talent and continuously engages with new emerging voices through our writing and engagement programmes. The Traverse is unique in Scotland in that it fulfils the crucial role of providing the infrastructure, professional support and expertise to ensure the development of a dynamic and vital theatre culture for Scotland. It is proud to continue in the spirit of innovation and risk-taking that first sparked its emergence and continues to engage with all sectors of society to increase access to the arts and promote lifelong learning. As we look to the future our ambition is to build on this extraordinary legacy; to invest in increased engagement with artists and audiences alike; and to continue to develop, produce and present world class drama for a national and international stage.

Company Biographies

Amiera Darwish (Tara)

Amiera Darwish's theatre credits include *Crime and Punishment* (Glasgow Citizens Theatre) and *Glasgow Girls* (National Theatre of Scotland). Television credits include *The Tunnel* (Sky Atlantic), *Waterloo Road* (BBC One), *Casualty* (BBC One) and *Scots Squad* (BBC Two). Film credits include *Kirk* (Dir. Michael Ferns).

Rob Jones (Assistant Director)

Rob Jones is a director and theatre maker based in Glasgow and London. He graduated in Theatre Studies from the University of Glasgow in 2010. His work on *Unfaithful* is supported by a Leverhulme Arts Scholarship as part of the James Menzies Kitchin Theatre Trust's Regional Directors Scheme. Rob's directing credits include *The Forbidden Experiment, Bonny Boys are Few, #neednothing* (Enormous Yes/The Arches) and *The Great Train Race* (A Play, A Pie and A Pint). His assisting credits include John Tiffany's *Macbeth* (National Theatre of Scotland). He was the recipient of the 2014 Platform 18 Award for new work at The Arches and was a participant in the National Theatre of Scotland's Emerge Programme 2012. Rob also works as a sound and video designer for theatre and his credits include *All The Sex I've Ever Had* (Mammalian Diving Reflex), *Thatcher's Children* (The Arches) and *Gate* (All Eyes Wide/Sonic-a).

Cara Kelly (Joan)

Theatre credits include: Florence in *The Odd Couple* (Perth Theatre); Winde Hinge in *The Hard Man* (Scottish Theatre Consortium); Lady Montague in *Romeo and Juliet* (Royal Lyceum Theatre); Maureen in *The Beauty Queen of Leenane* (Royal Lyceum Theatre); Duchess of Norfolk in *Henry VIII* (RSC); Elizabeth in *Elizabeth Gordon Quinn* (National Theatre of Scotland); Molly in *Molly Sweeney*, for which Cara won the Best Actress Critics Award for Theatre in Scotland (Citizens Theatre); Heather in *Loyal Women* (Royal Court); Dinah in *On Raftery's Hill* (Druid Theatre Co.); Pope Joan/Joyce in *Top Girls* (Old Vic, Stoke); Elizabeth I in *Mary Queen of Scots Got Her Head Chopped Off* (Prime Productions); Angela in *Sharp Shorts* (Traverse Theatre); Sarah in *Translations* (Donmar); Lady Macbeth in *Macbeth* (Brunton Theatre, Edinburgh); Virginia in *The Life of Galileo* (Almeida Theatre); Lucy/Mother/Mabel in *Young Playwrights Festival* (Royal Court); Kirstin in *Miss Julie* (Young Vic); Pegeen in *Playboy of the Western World* (Comminicado); Maud in *Steward of Christendom* (Out of Joint); Cordelia in *King Lear* (English Touring Theatre); Therese in *Therese Raquin* (Communicado); Dolly in *You Never Can Tell* (West Yorkshire Playhouse); Dorcas in *The Winter's Tale* (Young Vic); Linda in *All Things Nice* (Royal Court); Regina in *Ghosts* (Royal Lyceum); Mary in *Juno and the Paycock* (Royal Lyceum, Edinburgh). TV and Film Credits include: Margaret Henry in *Shetland* (BBC); Annie Wilson in *Waterloo Road* (BBC); Lucy Galbaith in *River City* (BBC Scotland); Agnes Williams in *Garrow's Law*

(BBC); Lorna in *Taggart* (STV); Librarian in *Rebus* (BBC); Catherine Macleod in *River City* (BBC); Dr. Lily Simkins in *Taggart* (STV); Miss Green in *Monarch of the Glen* (BBC); Kirsty in *State of Play* (BBC); Ann in *Superintendent Winter* (Sveriges TV); *Ultimate Force* (Bentley Productions); Dr. Giordano in *Life Support* (BBC); *Bramwell* (Bentley Productions) *The Bill* (Thames Television); Mary in *Precious Blood* (BBC); *Between the Lines* (ITV); *Doctor Finlay's Casebook* (ITV); Dawn in *Holy Cross* (BBC Film); Mary Doherty in *Sunday* (Channel 4 Film); Mother in short film, *Daddy's-gone-a-Fishing*.

Owen McCafferty (Playwright)
Over the past twenty years Owen McCafferty's plays have been performed throughout Europe and have won various awards. His work includes: *Quietly* (Abbey Theatre). This production transferred to the Traverse Theatre for the Edinburgh Festival 2013 and was awarded a Scotsman *Fringe First* and won the Writer's Guild Award for Best Play; *Titanic: Scenes from the British Wreck Commissioner's Inquiry 1912* (MAC, Belfast); *The Absence of Women* (Lyric Theatre, Belfast, and Tricycle Theatre, London); *Days of Wine and Roses* (Donmar, London); *Closing Time* (National Theatre, London); *Shoot the Crow* (Druid Theatre, Galway); *Cold Comfort* (Prime Cut Productions, Belfast); *Mojo Mickybo* (Kabosh, Belfast); and *Scenes from the Big Picture* (National Theatre, London), which won the Meyer-Whitworth, John Whiting and Evening Standard Awards: he is the only playwright to win these three major awards in one year for the same play. Owen's latest play, *The Death of a Comedian*, is to be produced by the Abbey Theatre in 2015.

Gary McCann (Designer)
Originally from County Armagh, Northern Ireland, Gary trained at Nottingham Trent University, and is now based in Greenwich, London. His design credits for theatre and opera include: *The Pitmen Painters* (National Theatre London, Volkstheater Vienna, Friedman Theatre Broadway), *The Girl in the Yellow Dress* (Market Theatre, Johannesburg, Stadttheater Stockholm, Baxter Theatre, Capetown), *The Barber of Seville*, *La Voix Humaine*, *L'Heure Espagnole* (Nationale Reisopera, Holland), *Die Fledermaus* (Norwegian National Opera), *The Flying Dutchman* (Ekaterinburg State Opera, Russia), *Three Days in May*, *Dangerous Corner* (West End, UK tours), *33 Variations* (Volkstheater Vienna), *Guys and Dolls* (Theater Bielefeld, Germany), *Fidelio* (Garsington Opera), *Cosi Fan Tutte* (Schönbrunn Palace, Vienna), *Norma* (National Opera of Moldova), *Imeneo* (London Handel Festival), *Faramondo* (Göttingen Festspiele Germany), *Owen Wingrave* and *La Pietra del Paragone* (Opera Trionfo, Amsterdam). Future projects from 2014 tp 2017 include: *Macbeth* (Vienna State Opera), *The Golden Cockerel* (Santa Fe Opera, New Mexico), *Turandot* (Chinese National Opera, Beijing), *L'Assedio di Calais* (Nationale Reisopera, Holland) and *La Traviata* (National Opera, Bucharest). His work has twice been exhibited at the V&A Museum in London – as part of the 'Collaborators' and 'Transformation/Revelation' exhibitions. www.garymccann.com

Rachel O'Riordan (Director)
Rachel is the Artistic Director of the Sherman Cymru Theatre. Prior to that she was at Perth Theatre, where her work included: *Cinderella, Macbeth, The Seafarer, Mother Goose, The Odd Couple* (*Female Version*), *Moonlight and Magnolias, Someone Who'll Watch Over Me* and *Twelfth Night*. Other work includes: *The Absence of Women* (Tricycle); *Hurricane* (West End/59E59 Off-Broadway); *Everything Is Illuminated* (Hampstead Theatre); *Miss Julie* and *Animal Farm* (Peter Hall Company, Theatre Royal, Bath); *Absolution* (Guna Nua/First Irish NY); *Much Ado About Nothing, The Glass Menagerie* and *Merry Christmas Betty Ford* (Lyric, Belfast); *A Christmas Carol, Gates of Gold* and *Grimm Tales* (Library Theatre, Manchester); *Over the Bridge* (Green Shoot/Waterfront Hall, Belfast); *Elizabeth – Almost By Chance a Woman* (Kabosh/Project, Dublin); *Protestants* (Soho Theatre, London); *Arguments for Terrorism* and *Cold Turkey at Nana's* (Òran Mór) Opera includes: *NI5* (new short operas) for Northern Ireland Opera at the MAC, Belfast. Rachel founded and was Artistic Director of Ransom, Belfast, for whom she commissioned and directed *National Anthem, Transparency, The Gentleman's Tea-Drinking Society, This Piece of Earth, The Early Bird, The Half* and *The Winners*. Ransom's work toured extensively across the UK and Ireland, and for the company she devised and ran a three-year programme, 'Write on the Edge', to develop female playwrights. Rachel has been an artist-on-attachment at the National Theatre Studio and a facilitating director on NT Connections. Awards and nominations include the Critics' Award for Theatre in Scotland Best Director and Best Ensemble for *The Seafarer*, 2013; Best Director for *Absolution* (First Irish Theatre Festival Awards, New York, 2010); nominated in the 2010 Irish Theatre Awards as Best Director for *Over the Bridge;* and as Best Director in the TMA Awards for *Much Ado about Nothing* and for *The Absence of Women* at the Lyric, Belfast. She was nominated in the 2012 CATS awards as Best Director for *Someone Who'll Watch Over Me* at Perth Theatre, which was also nominated for Best Actor and Best Ensemble. *Grimm Tales* for the Library Theatre, Manchester, was nominated as Best Family Show in the Manchester Evening News Awards, 2010. Other nominations include Best Touring Production (M.E.N.) for *Hurricane* and Best Production (Dublin Theatre Festival) for *Elizabeth*. Ransom's *The Gentlemen's Tea-Drinking Society* and *National Anthem* were nominated as Best New Play in the Irish Times Theatre Awards in 2009 and 2010 respectively.

Debra Salem (Sound Designer)
Debra Salem is a composer, sound designer, singer/songwriter and choir director. She composes for theatre, television, dance and radio and with over 60 professional commissions to her credit, and over the years she has collaborated extensively with many of Ireland's professional theatres and theatre companies including a commission for St Patricks Day festival (*Forty Songs of Green*) performed at the National Concert Hall in Dublin with Barabbas Theatre and a one-hundred-strong project choir. In Belfast, she was involved with many Lyric Theatre productions including *The Playboy of the Western World*, for which she underscored the entire play with live

original music written for classical and folk musicians. Other credits include *Little Foxes* (Leeds Playhouse), *Bold Girls* (7:84) and *Phedre* (Perth Theatre). Debra was the sound designer for the last two seasons at Perth Theatre with credits including *April in Paris*, *Macbeth*, *Blithe Spirit*, *The Odd Couple* and the award-winning *The Seafarer*. In 2012 Debra was commissioned by the Friends of William Soutar Society, along with pianist Paul Harrison and guitarist Kevin Mackenzie, to set to music and perform a number of Soutar's poems. The show, *The Sma Room Seance*, toured Scotland in May–June 2012 and is part of the Made in Scotland programme for the Edinburgh Fringe Festival 2014.

Kevin Treacy (Lighting Designer)
Theatre designs include: *The Shawshank Redemption* and *Dr Ledbetter's Experiments* (Edinburgh Fringe), *Theatre Brothel* (Almeida Festival, London), *Twelfth Night* (Nottingham Playhouse), *Beside the Sea* (Southbank Centre), *The Seafarer* (Perth Theatre and Lyric Theatre, Belfast), *Macbeth* (Perth Theatre and Tron Theatre Glasgow), *Blithe Spirit* (Perth Theatre), *The Nose* (The Performance Corporation; Irish Times Award for Best Lighting Design), *Drive-By* (Dublin Fringe Festival and Canterbury Festival), *The Yokohama Delegation* (Kilkenny Festival), *The Government Inspector* and *Arrah-na-Pogue* (Abbey Theatre, Dublin). Opera designs include: *The Flying Dutchman*, *The Bear, The Turn of the Screw*, *NI 5 Opera Shorts* and *Tosca* (NI Opera), *Imeneo*, *Rodelinda* (Royal College of Music), *Flavio*, *Xerxes*, and *La Tragédie de Carmen* (English Touring Opera), *Orpheus in the Underworld* (Scottish Opera, NI Opera), *Acis and Galatea*, *The Barber of Seville*, *Xerxes*, *La Cenerentola*, *The Kiss*, *Hansel and Gretel*, *Bastien and Bastienne* and *The* (*Little*) *Magic Flute* (Opera Theatre Company), *La Voix Humaine*, *Suor Angelica*, *The Medium* and *La tragédie de Carmen* (Wexford Festival Opera), *Orango* (Royal Festival Hall). www.kevintreacy.com

Owen Whitelaw (Peter)
Owen trained at the Royal Scottish Academy of Music and Drama. Previous credits for the Traverse Theatre include: *Cockroach* and *Rupture* (In co-production with the National Theatre of Scotland). Other theatre includes: *In Time O' Strife; Knives in Hens; Peter Pan; Mary Queen of Scots Got Her Head Chopped Off; Our Teacher's a Troll* and *365* (National Theatre of Scotland); Paul Bright's *Confessions of a Justified Sinner* (Untitled Projects Ltd/National Theatre of Scotland); *The Life of Stuff; Cotton Wool and Nowheresville* (Theatre 503); *Sleeping Beauty; King Lear* (Citizens Theatre); *Wonderland* (Vanishing Point/Edinburgh and Naples International Festival); *A Puff of Smoke* (Tristan Bates Theatre); *About a Goth; 10,000 Metres Deep* (Paines Plough/Òran Mór); *Romeo and Juliet* (Òran Mór). Film credits include: *Dying Light* (Rig Arts] for Dir. David Newbigging; *What Would Ridley Do* (Digital Guerillas); *Scoring* (short) for Dir. Evelina Honkanen; *After Waiting* (short) for Dir. Sean Yates; *Score* (short, dir. Richard Smith) and *7/11 in Repeat* (short, dir. Ivor Thomas). Radio credits include: *Mclevy*, *The Second Mr Bailey*, *Blindness* and *Acting Up* (BBC).

Benny Young (Tom)

Benny's recent theatre includes: *Macbeth* (Manchester International Festival/ Armory Park, New York); *Dear Scotland* (National Theatre of Scotland); *Philadelphia, Here I Come!* (London Donmar); *The Resistible Rise of Arturo Ui* (Chichester Festival Theatre/Duchess Theatre, West End); *The Seafarer* (Perth/Belfast Lyric); *27, A Christmas Carol, The Wheel, Be Near Me* and *Six Characters in Search of an Author* (all National Theatre of Scotland); *Moonlight and Magnolias, The Demon Barber, Jekyll and Hyde, Phedre, Faith Fall* (Oran Mor); David Leddy's *Sub Rosa* (Fire Exit Ltd, winner of a Herald Angel Award); *The Grapes of Wrath* (Chichester Festival Theatre/English Touring Theatre); *The Tobacco Merchant's Lawyer* (Glasgow Tron and Edinburgh Traverse); *Staircase, Address Unknown, Betrayed, Six Acts of Love* and *The Drawer Boy* (Glasgow Tron); *Night Time* (Traverse Theatre for the 2007 Edinburgh Fringe); and *Hughie* (Northern Irish and Scottish tour with the Arches Theatre Co). Previously he has toured the UK with The Touring Consortium in *The Crucible, A View from the Bridge* and *Hobson's Choice*, and spent seasons with the Royal National Theatre, the Royal Shakespeare Company, the Edinburgh Lyceum and The Wrestling School. He also appeared alongside Kevin Spacey in *The Iceman Cometh* at the Old Vic. Most recent television includes: *One Day Like This* (BBC); *Garrow's Law* (BBC); *Scottish Killers* (BBC); *Waking the Dead: Sins of the Father* (BBC); *Spooks* (BBC); *Talk to Me* (Company Pictures/ITV); and *Taggart: Genesis* (SMG). Earlier television includes two years as Brian Dunkley in *Coronation Street*; two years as DS Ted Hatchard in *Boon*; and guest roles in *Playing the Field; The Kid in the Corner; The Funny Man; The Bill; Between The Lines; Doctor Finlay; Family Affairs;* and *Tell Tale Hearts*. Feature films include: Hugh Hudson's *Chariots of Fire*, Sidney Pollock's *Out of Africa* and Taylor Hackford's *White Nights*.

Support the Traverse

We would like to thank the following corporate sponsors for their recent support

Alan Gray, Glass House Events
City Roomz, Edinburgh
Jury's Inn, Edinburgh

For their generous support, the Traverse thanks our Theatre Club Members

Lawnmarket

Katie Bradford, Fiona Campbell, Lawrence Clark, Iain Millar, Gillian Moulton, Helen Pitkethly, Nicholas Pryor

Grassmarket

Joan Aitken, Graeme Baillie, Richard Burtles, Mark Howitt, John Knight OBE, Judy McCulloch, Angus McLeod, Helen Ogilvy, Michelle Scott, Bridget Stevens, Kenneth CB Wilkie

Saltire 1

Jane Attias, Morven Brown, Stewart Brown, Richard A Buckland, Fiona Catherine Byrne, Ann Caldwell, Adrian Clark, Billy Differ, Anne Dignan, Elizabeth Drummond, Brian Ferguson, Ben Fletcher-Watson, Lynn Hamilton, Lynda K Haughney, Paul Holmes, Dale Idiens, Sadie McKinlay, Colin McWhannell, Willa McWhannell, Cathy Meils, Geraldine O'Riordan, Richard Parry, Cynthia Rahsman, Ed Rahsman, Mike Ridings, Ian Runacres, Susan Tritton, Peng Lee Yap

Thanks also to Penny and Alan Barr.

A special thanks to Stephen Cotton for his support over many years as Chair of the Traverse Theatre Board.

The Traverse Theatre's work would not be possible without the support of

Traverse Theatre – the Company

Mike Baillie	Acting Bar Manager
Calum Barnes	Marketing Assistant (Internship)
Emma Callander	Associate Director
Fiona Campbell	Box Office Manager
Jessica Chalmers	Box Office Supervisor
Linda Crooks	Executive Producer & Joint Chief Executive
Helen Davies	Marketing/Audience Development Manager
Claire Doohan	Marketing & Campaigns Officer
Claire Elliot	Deputy Electrician
Tom Grayson	Deputy Box Office Manager
David Greig	Associate Artist
Zinnie Harris	Associate Artist
Claire Layton	Box Office Supervisor
Kath Lowe	Front of House Manager
Lynsey Mackenzie	Receptionist/Administrative Assistant
Catherine Makin	Artistic Administrator
Kevin McCallum	Head of Production
Andy McNamee	Trainee Director and Engagement Artist
Ruth McEwan	Assistant Producer
Orla O'Loughlin	Artistic Director & Joint Chief Executive
Kate Park	Head of Marketing & Sales
Eleanor Pender	Press & Media Officer
Julie Pigott	Head of Finance & Administration
David Pollock	Operations Manager
Tim Price	Associate Artist
Pauleen Rafferty	Payroll & HR Officer
Sunniva Ramsay	Engagement Assistant
Renny Robertson	Chief Electrician
Michelle Sandham	Finance Officer
Tom Saunders	Lighting & Sound Technician
Gary Staerck	Head of Stage
Rosie Ward	Box Office Supervisor

Also working for the Traverse

Charlotte Anderson, Anastasia Athanasiou, Stephen Bangs, Colin Bell, Will Blake, Allie Butler, Emma Campbell, Irene Clarke, Ben Clifford, Amy Cloonan, Hannah Cornish, William Cuthbert, Koralia Daskalaki, Jonathan Dawson, Caitlin Delves, Catherine Elliot, Finn Den Hertog, Svetlana Dimcovic, Caro Donald, Rachel Duke, Jude Durnan, Katy Farlie, Beth Fraser, Andrew Gannon, Bridget George, Anna Ghazal, Anthony Gowling, Jessica Gregory, John Guest, Ryan Hamilton, Laura Hawkins, Helen Horne, Jenny Hulse, Laurence Irvine, Ian Jackson, Adam James, Rosie Kellagher, Jack Kinross, Francisca Martinez Garcia, Alan Massie, Cristina Matthews, Cleo McCabe, Bradley McCathie, Kieran McCruden, Mark McGrory, Kirsty McIntyre, Steve McMahon, Suzanne Mengiles Murray, Edwin Milne John Mitchell, Stephen Moir, William Moore, Hal Morrissey Gillman, Christine Nicholson, Cian O Siochain, Clare Padgett, Liam Pike, George Reid, Emily Reutlinger, Juan Rodriguez Gonzalez, Michelle Rolfe, Theodora Sakellaridou, Cassie Sibbin, Rosie Sim, Caitlin Skinner, Ashley Smith, Kat Smith, Joanne Sykes, Anna Thomson, Jessica Ward, Emma Whyte, Molly Wilson.

Traverse Theatre Board of Directors

Sir John Elvidge (Chair), Adrienne Sinclair Chalmers (Company Secretary)
Barbara Allison, Lynne Crossan, Roy McEwan, Adrian O'Donnell

Foreword

I vividly remember sitting down with Owen McCafferty last August. Over a drink, in the heady midst of full-on festival fever in the bar, he told me that he wanted to write a play for the Traverse.

Owen's hugely acclaimed play *Quietly*, produced by the Abbey Theatre in Dublin, was playing in Traverse 2 at the time. He explained that as a writer, the experience of having work on at the Traverse was a profound one. As a playwright he felt at home.

I was touched by Owen's honesty and delighted by his ambition. As the inevitable commission progressed and *Unfaithful* emerged I was arrested by his courage in casting such an unflinching and masterful eye on his subject matter.

I would especially like to thank our Guest Director Rachel O'Riordan for joining us on the *Unfaithful* journey and for responding with such clarity and conviction.

And of course it goes without saying that I thank Owen for making the Traverse an offer I couldn't refuse last August. And inviting me for that drink.

Orla O'Loughlin

Artistic Director, Traverse Theatre

Unfaithful

Over the last twenty years Owen McCafferty's plays have been performed throughout Europe and have won various awards. Previous work includes *Titanic* (*Scenes from the British Wreck Commissioner's Inquiry, 1912*), the inaugural performance at MAC, Belfast; *The Absence of Women* (Lyric Theatre, Belfast, and Tricycle Theatre, London); *Days of Wine and Roses* (Donmar Theatre); *Closing Time* (National Theatre, London); *Shoot the Crow* (Druid and Prime Cut Productions, Belfast); *Mojo Mickybo* (Kabosh); *Scenes from the Big Picture* (National Theatre, London, and Prime Cut Productions, Belfast), which won the Meyer-Whitworth, John Whiting and *Evening Standard* Awards; and *Quietly* (Abbey Theatre, Dublin), which won the Writer's Guild Award for Best Play. His latest play, *The Death of a Comedian*, is a co-production between Abbey Theatre, Lyric Theatre and Soho Theatre.

by the same author

from Faber

PLAYS ONE
(*Mojo Mickybo, Shoot the Crow, Closing Time, Scenes from the Big Picture, The Waiting List*)

TITANIC
(*Scenes from the British Wreck Commissioner's Inquiry, 1912*)
THE ABSENCE OF WOMEN
QUIETLY

from Nick Hern Books

ANTIGONE
(*after Sophocles*)
DAYS OF WINE AND ROSES
(*after J. P. Miller*)
COLD COMFORT
SCENES FROM THE BIG PICTURE
CLOSING TIME

from Lagan Press / Nick Hern Books

I WON'T DANCE DON'T ASK ME
THE WAITING LIST
SHOOT THE CROW
MOJO MICKYBO

from Lagan Press

THE PRIVATE PICTURE SHOW
FREEFALLING

from Tinderbox Theatre Company

NO PLACE LIKE HOME
THE CHAIRS
(*after Ionesco*)

libretto

MAY CONTAIN FLASH PHOTOGRAPHY

OWEN McCAFFERTY

Unfaithful

ff

FABER & FABER

First published in 2014
by Faber and Faber Limited
74–77 Great Russell Street
London WC1B 3DA

Typeset by Country Setting, Kingsdown, Kent CT14 8ES
Printed in England by CPI Group (UK) Ltd, Croydon, Surrey CRO 4YY

A CIP record for this book
is available from the British Library

ISBN 978–0–571–32186–5

FSC
www.fsc.org
MIX
Paper from
responsible sources
FSC® C013604

2 4 6 8 10 9 7 5 3 1

Unfaithful was first performed at the Traverse Theatre, Edinburgh, on 3 August 2014. The cast was as follows:

Tom Benny Young
Joan Cara Kelly
Tara Amiera Darwish
Peter Owen Whitelaw

Director Rachel O'Riordan
Designer Gary McCann
Lighting Designer Kevin Treacy
Composer and Sound Designer Debra Salem
Assistant Director Rob Jones

Characters

Tom
fifty-seven

Joan
fifty-five

Peter
twenty-eight

Tara
twenty-six

UNFAITHFUL

A hotel bar. Tara and Peter at a table. Tom is standing at the bar.

Peter i have to go

Tara don't go in tonight – stay here with me and have another drink

Peter don't do this

Tara stay and have another drink

Peter i can't

Tara you won't

Peter we agreed

Tara it shuts me out

Peter good – i do what i do – the money's there – no talk about it

Tara and if that's not working

Peter it is working – we agreed – didn't we agree

Tara i need to understand it or be part of it – i don't know

Peter do you like working in tesco's at the till day after day for fuck-all

Tara that's not it

Peter do you

Tara no

Peter that's all you need to understand – gathering money – it takes time

Tara stay

Peter this is just about work

Tara is it

Peter yes – i want to stay with you but i can't because i have to go to work – before i start into that i'm going to smoke a joint – alright – just let me do that

Tara right

Peter cool

Tara yeah – we agreed

Peter i might bring something back in the morning

Tara not a takeaway – don't want to eat another takeaway for breakfast

Peter there's no rules about time and food – how many people eat prawn curry for breakfast – very few – that's what makes it special – all about being special kid

Tara don't be bringing back prawn curry – nothing special about that just wrong

Peter have to go – you need money

Tara yeah

He hands her money. They kiss.

Peter i'm thinking kentucky fried maybe

He exits.

Tara counts the money. She checks Tom out then approaches him.

Tara is it ok if i stand here

Tom sure

Tara busy enough in here – this time of the day

Tom always a good crowd in after work

Tara so this is your local

Tom when i'm working in town yeah

Tara strange – hotel bar as your local

Tom should plumbers not drink in hotel bars

Tara plumbers can drink wherever they like

His phone rings.

Tom sorry

Joan enters the scene.

Joan hello

Tom well

Joan you finished the job

Tom aye – pain in the arse – you at home

Joan yeah – not long in – you heading home now

Tom going to have a few pints first

Joan the ones off the site with you

Tom nah – just standing here on my own

Joan i'll wait before i put something on then

Tom aye

Joan you want fish

Tom aye fish

Joan see you later

Tom aye see you later

Joan exits.

Tara was that your wife checking up on you

Tom she wasn't checking up on me – are you waiting on someone

Tara sorry – sometimes i say things i shouldn't – no i'm not waiting on anyone – i was sitting in the corner and i saw you standing alone and thought i'd like to buy you a pint – would you like a pint – my name's tara by the way

Tom tom – it's ok i have one in front of me

Tara when you've finished that one i'll buy you another

Tom maybe

Tara maybe

Tom i mightn't want any more after i finish this one

Tara you told your wife you were going to have a few beers

Tom and what

Tara i've been watching you – that's only your first pint

Tom watching me

Tara not in a bad way – i'm not going to leave a bullet wrapped up in my knickers taped to the windscreen of your car

Tom van

Tara right – that changes things then – do you know where i can get some knickers – you looked interesting so i thought i'd buy you a pint that's all

Tom looked interesting

Tara a working man drinking in a hotel bar – that's interesting

Tom all i'm doing is having a pint

Tara same here – if your wife phoned back now would you still say you were on your own

Tom i don't understand – are you at work here

Tara am i a hooker

Tom yes – because i'm not interested

Tara no

Tom right – look – i've just finished a hard day's graft – i'm working in what used to be a beautiful old building but which some shit-head has now converted into poxy little apartments – i've been plumbing toilets all day – and because all tilers are dickheads it's taking me longer than it should – plus my mouth's full of dust because all the labourers are lazy bastards who won't sprinkle water over the place – i thought i'd have a few pints on the way home – clear my throat – so i'm standing here on my own . . .

Tara i bet your wife doesn't know you drink here does she – she thinks you drink in some male shit-hole with your workmates

Tom sometimes i do – i stand here on my own have a few pints then go home – no one bothers me – it suits me to do that

Tara me talking to you is annoying then

Tom i've had a hard day at work and if i'm going to talk to someone i don't want that someone to be crazy – strange – you know – bullets in the knickers – asking about my wife – knowing how many pints i've had

Tara do you want to talk about the weather

Tom no

Tara we could just stand here and drink – not talk – do you want another drink

Tom no – i have enough here

Tara let me buy you one

Tom i'm fine

Tara are you the type of man that doesn't let women buy him drink

Tom no – i'm a big fan of women buying me drink – but only when i need one

Tara a man of discipline

Tom i don't see the point in having more than you need

Tara so your wife – would you now say you were with somebody or you were alone

Tom i'd tell her i was alone

Tara good

Tom why

Tara just better that's all

Tom right

Tara don't you think

Tom maybe

Tara ask me something

Tom what do you do

Tara i'm a student – was a student – dropped out – i'm a dropout

Tom my daughter julie's a student

Tara what's she do

Tom something to do with business – she moved out – we don't see her a great deal – i think she likes it though – well she never says she doesn't – so – finishes next year – her mother's hoping she'll move back in – she won't though – why would she – a young woman wants to be out there on her own

Tara do you want her to move back

Tom don't know – it's good having the house to ourselves – the only problem with that is we've grown out of the way of being alone with each other – anyway fuck that – why'd you drop out

Tara got bored

Tom what did you do

Tara maths

Tom sums

Tara aye sums

Tom you got bored so you just stopped

Tara i'm allowed to do that – we live in a free world

Tom a free world – if everybody that got bored dropped . . .

Tara i saw a man in a bar i thought i might like to talk to – adult to adult – i'm not your child

Tom you could be

Tara i can't help that

Tom why'd you get bored

Tara i don't know

Tom you can't not know – if you don't know it's nonsense

Tara alright

Tom i'm just saying

Tara i was standing in tesco's buying some fruit – i eat a lot of fruit because i think it's good for me – makes me a healthier person – i was looking at the checkout girl – she was about the same age as me – i was looking at her working or living or something – i don't know i just thought what the fuck am i doing – next thing i was at a lecture – sitting there looking at the guy giving the lecture – just watching his mouth open and close – his big mouth flapping – his trousers were an inch too short and his shirt wasn't ironed – i thought nobody cares about you – no one cares about you and you're telling me what to do – fuck that – all this pretending – pretending what i was doing was a real thing that mattered – it didn't – it doesn't – i didn't understand why i was there so i just left

Tom just got up and left

Tara i got up from my seat – packed my books away – told the lecturer i was sorry – left the lecture hall – and walked straight into the toilets and masturbated

Tom ok – right

Tara are you embarrassed by that

Tom yes – sort of

Tara sorry

Tom is that what you want

Tara yes sort of – it was brilliant – the masturbating

Tom good – i'm glad

Tara being on your own – totally on your own – forget about what's expected of you and just do something for yourself – it's a beautiful feeling – you ever felt that

Tom so you left then

Tara yes

Tom just left and that's that

Tara just left and that's that

Tom you'll go back

Tara i won't

Tom you feel that way now but . . .

Tara don't lecture me

Tom if you want to talk with me you have to let me talk – whenever my daughter said she was going to university i had mixed feelings about it – part of me was glad because you always want your child to have better opportunities than you did – going to university opens doors – another part of me was more apprehensive – apprehensive because you don't want your own child to end up with their head stuck up their own arse – lose the fucking guff – if i'm interesting it's because to you i might look as if i might know something not because i'm a plumber standing in a fucking hotel bar

Tara sorry – and your daughter's head – is it stuck up her own arse

Tom not yet – but i'm sure there's time

Tara i don't want to go back – i want to do something different

Tom like what

Tara don't know – maybe be an assistant to a plumber

Tom you don't want to spend your time doing that

Tara why not

Tom because i've spent my time doing it – and you end up saying why the fuck did i spend my time doing that

Tara you should spend your time doing something else then

Tom it doesn't work like that

Tara there's no rules

Tom at my age there is

Tara do you want to fuck me

Tom is that why we're talking

Tara from the first time i looked at you it was always a possibility – it's not the only reason though – do you want to fuck me

Tom you don't have to say that

Tara i know i don't – i want to

Tom really you don't have to say it – it's not expected

Tara i know that – believe me – look i'll put it another way – if you want to fuck me you can – you don't have to say now this second

Tom look i'm not sure that . . .

Tara it doesn't matter – if you say no it's alright – i won't leave with my tail between my legs if you don't want to put your tail between my legs – you see the way i used humour there to try and get you round to my way of thinking

Tom i like you

Tara is that a yes

Tom part of me wants to trail you into the nearest doorway

Tara what does the other part want to do

Tom trail you into the nearest doorway

Tara and what – say it

Tom fuck you

Tara there must be doorways about here somewhere

Tom there's another part

Tara there doesn't have to be another part

Tom there does

Tara alright – look listen – if i say this you'll believe me right

Tom right

Tara i know what i'm doing – i know what i'm doing and i want to do it – i am not in a bad place at the moment – this is not about me punishing myself by fucking some old man

Tom thank you

Tara you're welcome – i have no problem with my own father – i won't call you daddy – i saw you standing on your own and i wanted to meet you – all i'm saying is if you wanted to fuck me that would be a good thing

Tom look i am not . . .

Tara sorry one more thing – i do not in any way care that you are married – i will not be a problem – as we have already established it's not a bullet and knickers thing

Tom i don't care about any of that stuff

Tara what then

Tom i'm not a casual person

Tara can we not just . . .

Tom are you going to listen to me

Tara yes daddy – that was a joke

Tom i like the way you talk to me – i like the fact that you're standing here talking to me at all – it feels like something i need

She kisses him.

look we'll have another drink here then i've to go

Tara stay with me longer than one more drink

Tom shall we go somewhere else – go for a walk – have a drink after that

Tara a walk

Tom yeah

Tara a real walk

Tom yeah – it'll be good – it's getting dark – the city will be lit up

Tara ok

Tom we can stay here if you want – i'm just saying – you know – a dander about the town and then another few drinks

Tara i'd love to go for a walk around town with you – look for a doorway

The following evening. Joan and Tom at home.

Joan that's it – no answer – nothing – silence – fuck – why – i need to know – what it is you do – cry – tell a joke – whisper i love you – do you hate me – oh god – is this the – it is isn't it – it's the it isn't you it's me fucking thing – you poor child – little lost and lonely soul – i want to know why

Tom i don't know why

Joan you owe me

Tom i owe you fuck all – i've been here too – all this time

Joan don't hide – be a man

Tom be a man

Joan yes – treat me with respect

Tom as a man the answer is – because she was there

Joan i want to know why you need to be with other women

Tom one other woman

Joan how do i know that

Tom why would i lie

Joan because you can – because you have

Tom one other woman

Joan just in case i'll assume that the reason for fucking one is the same reason for fucking many

Tom what does any of that matter – it's done

Joan it's done – that it – it's done

Tom i met a woman – we had sex – you found out about it – it's done

Joan we have to talk about this

Tom no we don't

Joan i want to talk

Tom i don't

Joan why did you do it

Tom i don't know why

Joan something must've been happening – why didn't you tell me

Tom because that's what we do – we don't tell each other things

Joan why didn't you try and change that then – do something different – why didn't you ask me – tell me the situation – see what my reaction might've been

Tom don't be bloody stupid – i know damn well what your reaction would've been

Joan no you don't

Tom what are you saying – i should've phoned up – i should've said to you – there's a woman i've just met – i didn't seek her out by the way – i just met her – there's a woman i've just met and she's said something kind to me

Joan have the conversation with me – say it to me now

Tom no

Joan why not

Tom	because it's bloody stupid
Joan	it's not – it might do some good
Tom	what bloody good
Joan	have the fucking conversation – right – so we're on the phone
Tom	how's it goin
Joan	alright – alright
Tom	you get all your work done
Joan	nearly – when will you be home
Tom	i'm going to have a few beers first
Joan	ok – you on your own – are you on your own
Tom	no
Joan	who's there
Tom	i'm talking to this women
Joan	who is she
Tom	i don't know
Joan	you don't normally talk to women you don't know
Tom	no
Joan	what are you talking about
Tom	nothing
Joan	what
Tom	this is what this is about – you don't care that i fucked someone else – you care that i talked to them

Joan no – believe me i care that you fucked someone else

Tom we're talking about me

Joan what about you

Tom she said i looked like a man

Joan did she now

Tom i don't often hear that – it's good to be told you look like a man

Joan what age is she

Tom what has that got to do with anything

Joan don't pretend you don't know that's important

Tom it's not about you

Joan you see the way you say something then your nostrils open up – i fucking hate that – and when you come to bed at night – when you're taking your socks off you make that grunting noise – i fucking hate that too – sometimes i lie in bed at night listening to you breathe – only i haven't the courage i'd put a pillow over your head and hold it there until your feet stopped kicking – the way you chew your food – rub your nose – pick your ears – it all makes me sick – sometimes when you touch me my skin crawls – you're stinking breath everywhere – i wouldn't mind if it was worth it but it's not – and on top of that you're now a liar – don't tell me what's about me and what's not about me – what age is she

Tom how do i know what age she is – make-up – all that crack

Joan what fucking age is she

Tom mid-thirties – older woman are all mad

Joan yes – they've been around older men too long

Tom that was a deal breaker for me – whether she was mad or not – had to set her a test and everything – she nearly won a washing machine

Joan don't try and be cute – save that for the barstool – what is it you wanted to ask me

Tom i have this feeling that if this woman keeps talking to me the way she is at the moment i'm going to want to fuck her – what do you think about that – do you think that's a good idea – what do you think

Joan what's she like

Tom she has a beard – so what do you think joan – can i fuck her – is it ok

Joan how are you going to fuck her – the back of the van – give her one in the back of the van – never fucked me in the back of the van – oh no

Tom this is stupid

Joan keep fucking going

Tom she says to me do you want to fuck me – i say yes – we finish our drinks and we go outside – the street's busy – that turns me on – everyone going about their business –

and in amongst that there's this woman who wants me – i kiss her – funny thing about that is she kisses me back – we walk up some alleyway – holding hands – we pass a doorway – i grab her by the hair and pull her into it – i bite her – just enough to draw blood from her lip – she unzips my trousers kneels down and sucks my cock – she makes that noise – the noise women make when they like sucking cock – she stops before i cum – we kiss again – i put my hand up her skirt – i ran my fingers along her thigh then slip them down inside her pants – i finger-fuck her while sucking her nipples – she cums – she takes her pants off and lifts her skirt up – i bend her over kneel down behind her and lick her cunt – while i'm doing that i stick one of my fingers up her ass – she cums again – i stand up and fuck her from the back – just before i cum i pull out and shoot over her ass – she puts her pants back on and i pull my trousers up – we go back out on to the street – we kiss again and then she leaves – hello – hello – are you still there joan – did you get all that

Joan did you only fuck her the once – poor woman

Tom very good

Joan why don't you do all those things with me – you could've said something – we could've talked about it – we could've gone down that road together – know what i hate about you – you're fucking stupid – not stupid in that you're thick –

stupid as in you're fucking scared – all you had to do was talk – how can you look at me and not know i have those thoughts – if you have them i have them – why the fuck didn't you do this ten years ago – maybe you did

Tom once – right once – and i didn't choose the timing

Joan yes you did

Tom ten years ago – now – what the hell difference does it make

Joan ten years ago i could've done something – i could've changed my life – not now – i'm beyond that now – i've been left behind – that's where the cheating part comes in – i feel i've been cheated – not cheated on – but cheated of – cheated of time – jesus christ you can't even fuck-up properly

Tom where are you going

Joan don't waste your breath

A few hours later. Joan and Peter in a hotel room.

Joan i feel – i feel stupid saying this but i haven't done this before

Peter that makes two of us

Joan jesus – seriously

Peter no – i've done this many times – many many times – don't worry

Joan worried – i'm not worried – i'm curious – not worried

Peter curious – don't often hear that from clients – it's cool though – i can do curious

Joan clients – i'd feel a bit – happier – if we maybe eased our way into this

Peter of course – would you like me to pour you a drink

Joan why not – one more won't hurt

Peter a gin and tonic

Joan yes a gin and tonic – well remembered – are you going to have one

He goes to the mini-bar.

Peter i don't normally

Joan put you off your stroke does it – sorry – that was – after me saying we should ease our way in there – i just – jumped in

Peter don't worry it's ok – no not really

Joan what

Peter no not really – it doesn't put me off my stroke

Joan not really

Peter not at all – i just don't normally – that's all

Joan i'd prefer if we did – share something

Peter ok – i'll have a beer

Joan cheers

Peter cheers

Joan i'm going to sound stupid again

Peter i'm sure you won't – and even if you do it's fine – you can sound whatever way you want

Joan stop doing that

Peter stop doing what

Joan agreeing with everything i say – being overly pleasant to me – i'm not up here to be pampered – that isn't what this is about – what i mean is – you can be who you are

Peter you're going to pay me to be who i am

Joan no – i'm going to pay you to fuck me – but in the run-up to that i'd prefer if you were to be who you are – unless of course who you are is a complete nutter – then i'd prefer if you hid it

Peter i'll try

Joan the thing i was going to say – the stupid thing – it will just be silly really – oh god i wish i could shut up

Peter look

Joan joan

Peter look – joan

Joan and what's your name – your real name – not something you use for business – like – long john – or – king – i don't know king something – king kong – king kong with the massive dong

Peter peter

Joan right – peter

Peter you can say whatever you want to me – you don't have to apologise about anything ever – anything you want – you can be abusive if you want – don't worry about that

Joan i need you to know who i am – i don't want to come over all motherly here – like i'm going to say to you – look son you shouldn't really be doing this to yourself – ultimately it's degrading and you should really try and make a better life for yourself – you see you may look at me and think that that's me and that that's what i'm doing here – talking to you like this – the point is i don't care how you ended up here and where you move on to afterwards – all i'm saying is i'd prefer if we talked first – there's nothing more to it than that – no hidden agenda

Peter sometimes it can be more difficult for clients joan to operate within this situation if they attempt to make the relationship more personal than it actually is – which is why i don't normally take a drink – i'm only pointing this out to you as a possible risk – we will of course do whatever you want

Joan look if you're totally against the idea just say so

Peter we have to get this straight here – this is a business deal – a deal which i want to complete – if you want to talk we'll talk

Joan you sounded very businesslike there – in a good way – a firm handshake type of way – once the deal is struck the deal is struck – i'm not the type of man to go back on my word type of thing

Peter i am a businessman – and i'm not the type of man to go back on his word

Joan do you have a pimp – that sounded funny – a pimp – it felt like i was in an episode of kojak

Peter really

Joan do you know what that is

Peter no

Joan i told you don't do that – if you're here to do what i want – stop doing that

Peter i'm part of an escort agency

Joan what are you escorting me to

Peter the end

Joan we'll see – many a woman has been told that – because you say it doesn't make it true – so you pay money to this escort agency the same way a taxi driver pays rental to the depot

Peter something like that

Joan my daughter studies business at university – this is her final year

Peter does she enjoy it

Joan i think so – she doesn't really tell us much – she's going through that stage where she thinks she's better than we are – her father's a plumber and i'm a dinner lady – she thinks we don't know anything – which is true – we don't know anything – but she doesn't know that

Peter what type of business is she interested in

Joan to be honest i don't know

Peter maybe one day she'll open up her own escort agency

Joan maybe she will – maybe when she's doing the monthly accounts she'll find my name at the bottom of a cheque – that would be funny – assuming i get used to all this – which i won't – i have the feeling this is a one-off thing

Peter can i say something

Joan yes

Peter i see you as a woman – a woman i don't know – i don't care what age you are – i don't care about your race your religion or your politics – i don't care that you're married – that you're a mother – and that you may see me as a young man that has lost his way – all that i care about is that you have enough money to pay me and that you're not dissatisfied with the product i'm selling

Joan that's the most liberating thing a man has ever said to me – it turns me on – i know i'm doing the right thing now – my husband had sex with another woman – he met her in this very hotel – i'm returning to the scene of the crime – do you get that a lot with women my age – revenge fucks

Peter not as much as you'd imagine

Joan do you get many women my age

Peter my fair share

Joan i have a feeling that it was his first time – not that i let him away with that – maybe i only think that because this is my first time – i thought coming here i'd get back at him – we've been married a long time – and it's just – it made me think what was the point of it all – you know – what it feels like – that we had gone through life together – and that maybe we had reached a point or something – we had both reached the same point – and that we were questioning our life together – and that he acted on that and he didn't tell me – it wasn't that he did it or felt like that but that he didn't tell me – you see we could've said to each other – look this is a moment where we agree to break free from each other – break free once – and then come back together – fuck him – fuck him – he's a wee tosspot isn't he – and by the way this is one of those times when you can ignore what i previously said and agree with me

Peter he's a wee tosspot

Joan a wise choice

Peter but

Joan but what – no brotherhood nonsense – no all for one and one for all – it's my money in that purse not his

Peter you wanted me to talk

Joan i did – sorry about the money thing

Peter don't be – if you felt like that why didn't you say to him

Joan it was only after i found out about him that i considered that to be an option – maybe that's it – he didn't think about me – he said to me – this isn't about you – i could've thought solely about myself – and didn't – and he did – there's another thing that's fucking annoying me – our sex life – is – you know what at this moment i don't care – does your mother know you do this for a living – that was a joke

Peter i'm not going to tell you who i am and why i'm here

Joan you could lie

Peter i thought you wanted me to be me

Joan we're still ourselves when we lie – do you like what you do

Peter do you

Joan oh fuck off

Peter there are parts of it i like more than others

Joan like what

Peter i'm not mad keen on giving old men blowjobs

Joan neither am i

Peter do you like slopping out shitty meals to kids

Joan i don't slop shitty meals out any more – i'm the supervisor – i organise what shitty meals to slop out – but just so you get the image right in your head – so i've been told – it's – nylon pinnies with no skirt on underneath – flip flops – and on cold days a pair of your husband's socks – is that how you remember the dinner ladies when you were at school

Peter i always brought my own lunch

Joan i thought that was going to lead somewhere

Peter yes – sorry – yes it's how i remember them – and even though i brought a lunch with me i'd still go round to look at the dinner ladies – they had no knickers on – that's the way i always thought of them – no knickers – easier to get at

Joan not dinner ladies

Peter i take it supervisors dress differently – a bit more stylish – but still no knickers – still easy to get at

Joan supervisors dress – they wear – they wear – fuck this – i don't care how supervisors dress – they dress – i'll tell you how they dress – like people who have passed their fucking sell-by date but haven't fucking recognised that yet – this is stupid – how much do i owe you

Peter you want me to leave now

Joan how much do i owe you

Peter we have already discussed prices

Joan how much – i want to hear you say it again – this is a business deal so i want to hear you say the amount

Peter alright – for the amount of time i've spent here – i don't know – give me eighty quid

She does.

that's us finished then

Joan yes

He gets himself a drink and puts the money for it on the mini-bar. He sits down and takes a drink.

Peter i'm not a refugee who has crossed the seas in a fucking bathtub to escape a life of misery and deprivation – i don't live in a squat with nineteen other people all shitting into the same bowl and beating the fuck out of each other to see who gets the last piece of bread – while we all wait for a man in a limo to come each evening and pick the lucky ones – i'm not an addict – i don't need to swallow pints of spunk to feed my addiction – having to inject myself time and again in order to drift off into oblivion so i don't have to confront my own guilt – nor sadly to say was i ever abused as a child – deprived of my self-worth – and the only thing i know to do – the only thing that makes me feel that there might be any applause after it's finished – is to fuck or to be fucked – nor am i putting myself through college to eventually become a lawyer – is there anything i missed out do you think

Joan you could be paying off a gambling debt to the people who run the prostitution racket

Peter nor am i paying off a gambling debt to the people who run the prostitution racket – nor do i live in a gangster movie where all the prostitution rackets are

Joan so there's no story to tell – there must be something that allows you to give old men blowjobs

Peter there is – a freedom of spirit that allows me to embrace capitalism in any way shape or form

Joan that isn't a story

Peter do you want to know what happened

Joan yes – i'm going nowhere

Peter i'm an out-of-work actor that was told a year or so ago that my talents may best be suited to either modelling or porn movies – i didn't make any headway with the modelling – and i can't understand why – given my delightfully high cheekbones – so i made one – not widely distributed – porn movie – to be honest i felt maybe my heart wasn't really in it – i felt maybe i needed a more one-to-one atmosphere – and also i wanted to be my own boss – so i took to the streets – and here i am now in a hotel room

Joan why do you want to make a fool of me – go on – fuck off – leave

Peter i was working in a call centre earning fuck-all and having people bitch in my ear all day long – i withdrew into myself – i didn't go out – so i didn't meet anyone – i hadn't had sex in a long time – i paid a prostitute – i got talking to her about how much she earned – she said because i had a big cock i could earn some good money – she put me in contact with someone – and here i am

Joan i don't want you to go – can i ask you to do specific things

Peter yes

Joan right – right

Peter it's fine – say it

Joan i want you to fuck me up the ass – hard – fuck me up the ass hard

Peter is that what you like

Joan i don't know – i've never done it before

Peter ok

Joan no wait – i want to abuse you first – verbally – you said that was ok

Peter i did

Joan i don't know how to start this

Peter just start it – you stupid old cunt

Joan you useless worthless no-dick ugly fucker piece of shit fuckin cunt – stupid fuckin cunt – moron – fucking moron – stupid selfish moron fuckin cunt – fuckin bastard – you think you just need to smile and that's enough you fuckin cunt – i hate you – blind bastard – cock for brains – one other cock among the many – nameless – faceless – just another man – nothing special – you all eventually fall into fucking line – sheep – all think you're peacocks strutting your stuff and you're all just fucking sheep – every fuckin one of you – all full of plans – life plans – stuff – life – fuckin cunts – just waiting all the time for someone to suck your dick – stupid fucker – women should be told – from the very start all of you should say – i'm blind – i know it doesn't seem like that but i am – it's a certain type of blindness – i only see what i want to fucking see – should rip your eyes out and make you blind proper you cunt – i know you think that in some way that you're charming and funny and kind and understanding and a pleasure to be with – the truth is you exhaust me – you just fucking exhaust me

Peter that it

Joan yes – this isn't easy for me you know – after a certain age you lock your body away – never to be seen by a stranger again

The following morning. Tom has slept in a chair beside the bed. Joan enters.

Tom where have you been

Joan out

Tom out

Joan i booked into an hotel for the night

Tom an hotel

Joan why – where did you think i was going to sleep – a park bench – maybe i should've dossed out in a doorway with the homeless

Tom you could've stayed with julie

Joan well i didn't

Tom have you had anything to eat

Joan no

Tom was there no breakfast at the hotel – hotels normally do breakfasts – they're known for that type of thing

Joan angry because i was out on my own is that it

Tom no

Joan i booked into an hotel – and no i didn't eat the breakfast – i didn't feel like anything to eat

Tom right

Joan yes – right

Tom are you going to go to work

Joan no

Tom right

Joan are you

Tom no

Joan excellent we can spend the day together – any ideas what to do

Tom sit in silence

Joan i don't think so

Tom i didn't have sex with her

Joan what

Tom i didn't have sex with her

Joan what do you mean – you didn't fuck her – the two of you just fooled around or something

Tom fooled around – i'm not fourteen – we didn't do anything together – nothing

Joan i don't understand this – i don't . . .

Tom listen . . .

Joan don't tell me to listen

Tom i'm going to say – i met this woman in a bar

Joan she does actually exist then

Tom of course she exists – we got to talking – we had a bit of a laugh . . .

Joan no no no – this is you trying to get out of it – isn't it – you've sat up all night thinking about this – and this was the best plan you could come up with

Tom there is no plan

Joan accept the blame for something – then when the dust settles say you didn't do it – make yourself the victim – it's what men do – was i meant to put you through more hell than i did – i was wasn't i – i was to make this whole situation into a nightmare for you – then you say you didn't do anything – and you don't know why you said what you did – and because that is a lesser crime you get away with it – in fact it might even make you seem colourful – then i feel guilty – when in actual fact you did fuck her – i apologise – i'm sorry that last night i didn't make you feel bad enough – do you want me to do that now – would that make the situation easier for you

Tom stop it – there's no damn plan

Joan don't tell me to fucking stop anything – i want to make this situation better for you – tilt the glaring white light that is shining on your bare arse over to me

Tom don't do this joan – i didn't sleep with her – that's the truth

Joan nice try – you lying little cunt – you know what i did last night – after i booked into the hotel i had a bath – shaved my legs – put my best make-up on – i took my time over that – i wanted to look my best – then i went down and sat in the bar and had a few drinks – there were two men standing at the other end of the bar – i went down and talked to them – we all got on well – having a laugh – i didn't want to be too in their faces about it – i didn't want to put them under any pressure you know – maybe they had other things to do – more important things – maybe they were businessmen that were going to a late night meeting or something – so i said to them look if you don't fancy this it's fine – here's my room number – i'll spare you the details – i was going to call you – but then i thought – no – he wouldn't be into it – you were never much of a sharer – you happy now – that fit into your plan a bit more

Tom i didn't have sex with her

Joan why would you let me think you did then

Tom i don't know

Joan i've been with you all this time – here – over thirty years – beside you

Tom to annoy you – all that you-owe-me shit – you just jumped straight in there

Joan to annoy me – to fucking annoy me

Tom to hurt you – in order to feel something i had to hurt you – you're the only one i can hurt – the only one – i don't know

Joan why does anyone need to be hurt tom

Tom oh fuck off – don't pretend you don't know what that might mean

Joan i sat in the hotel room on my own – had a few drinks – then i just lay on top of the bed

Tom it's just the two of us – here – now

Joan yes

Tom no need to lie

Joan yes

Tom i didn't do anything

Joan neither did i

Silence.

Tom look – i – i don't know what the hell is happening to me – i don't know how to be – and i'm not even sure what that fucking means – in my head i'm fighting with everything – all the time – can't relax – can't read a paper – can't watch the news – the tv's a lot of fuckin nonsense – don't know why i'm going to work – resent the money i get – don't want to talk to anyone – can't fuckin sleep – i have this feeling that every minute of the day i'm hounded – all the time – everything – i went into this shop to buy a sandwich for lunch the other day – there must have been about twenty types – couldn't pick one – even that was beyond me – just stood there looking at all these fucking sandwiches – i didn't care and because i didn't care i couldn't pick one – i'm standing looking at these fuckin sandwiches and on top of that – i know – i am aware – that there's people starving in the world – and on top of that i know that i can't really do anything about that so i should just buy a sandwich – and on top of that i know there are people starving in the world – and on and on – every time i see an old photograph or watch a clip from an old movie all that i can think of is that all those people are dead – every one of them fucking dead – i read this thing in a magazine about the earth's magnetic force or core or something flipping over and it wiping everything out – no trace of us – no fucking trace of us – nothing – nothing – not a fucking trace – all fucking day i spent looking at a piece of copper pipe and thinking that – all that wasted time – all time wasted – and fucking on and on and on – and then there's you – what are we doing – i don't know what the fuck we are doing – it used to be that we just existed or something – and that seemed alright – and now i don't know if that's enough – or there should be more – or fucking less – is this a natural thing i'm going through – we're going through – is this the way it is for everyone – and all those things you said about me i think about you – and even if i don't really believe them they're floating about there somewhere – you see – this – this is what this is all about – you and i have been together all this time – side by side breathing each other's air – is this it – is this fucking it

Joan you're such a dickhead

Joan grabs Tom by the hair and pulls his face towards hers. She kisses him

fuck me

The same morning. Tara and Peter's flat.

Peter enters. He has a takeaway. Tara is just off the phone. She hasn't slept.

Peter hi

Tara hi

They kiss.

Peter who was on the phone

Tara no one

Peter no one

Tara my mother

Peter how is she

Tara same – usual

Peter was she asking for me

Tara not really

Peter nice – did you tell her

Tara no – she wanted to know when i was going over to see her

Peter you should tell her

Tara don't be stupid – i'll maybe take the bus over on monday evening

Peter do you want me to go with you – i could take the night off

Tara no i don't want you to go with me

Peter i'm not marked – she'll not know just by looking at me

Tara we both know you'd find a way of showing her your badge – it's not important

Peter whatever – you're right it's not important – i'm wrecked

Tara you shouldn't work so hard

Peter i'm the best child in the class – i do who i'm told

He hands her money.

you lodge that later today

Tara yeah

Peter take some if you need it

Tara i don't need any

Peter we always need money – i brought breakfast

Tara i'm not hungry

Peter your favourite – king prawn thai yellow curry

Tara i like it in the evening when normal people eat it

Peter not this again – and by the way whenever we first met did i not now and again eat takeaway shit in the morning

Tara hungover – back to front is alright when you're hungover

Peter i'm tired – alright we'll eat later – closer to lunchtime – less chance of us getting raided by the food police then – what time's your shift at

Tara i'm not going in today

Peter have you phoned in or do you want me to do it

Tara no it's ok i'll do it later – i was thinking i might need a change anyway – i was standing behind the counter the other day –

wednesday – the queue at my till was a mile long – all the queues were a mile long – sometimes it feels like it's never going to end – normally i try and talk to each customer – passes the time – i kept looking at the queue and thinking it's never going to end – then all i could see was the groceries – each individual thing – thousands of them – all making that bleeping noise – bleep bleep bleep – that's the only thing i could hear – but not just from my till but from every till – meaningless fucking noise – didn't know what i was doing there – i told that weasel of a supervisor i was ill – got changed – walked about the town – then went and had a drink on my own – i'm not happy there

Peter leave – get another job – move on

Tara i might go to night school or something

Peter why

Tara do something different – i don't know – i was watching this documentary the other day – it was about maths – and how maths influences nearly every aspect of our lives – and i sort of understood it – i didn't understand it all – i thought maybe i should try and understand more of it – so i might go back to school – try and get to university maybe

Peter you'd be better off doing something like business studies or something – better chance of getting a job out of it

Tara business studies – i work as a checkout in a supermarket – and i'm going to leave to do business studies – so i can end up back at the supermarket but this time as a supervisor – i don't think so

Peter you could end up running your own business – start up your own escort agency – employ me

Tara that would be a move up from the supermarket alright

Peter that would be a good laugh wouldn't it – you on the phone to me – hey peter – pick up this oul doll down in the hotel bar – you probably don't remember her – she says she's been with you before and she wants you again – because you're that good – by the way when you're finished could you pick something up for dinner on the way home – whatever – do what you want to do darlin – whatever makes you happy

Tara i'll maybe find out what courses there are

Peter you do that – if you're not going to work today i'll maybe take the night off – the two of us can just sit here all day and get stoned

Tara there's no blow left – i couldn't sleep so i smoked it

Peter i'm not going out to get any – i'm knackered – you go

Tara why don't we just go to bed

Peter ok we'll get the blow later – if we're going to have a fuck i need to take a pill – you know the score – there's time involved there – do you want me to take the pill

Tara no peter i don't want you to take a fucking pill – twenty-eight years of age and you have to take a fucking pill because you're stressed out because of all the other hard-ons

Peter i'm not stressed out

Tara are you not

Peter no i'm not

Tara well you should be

Peter i can't just perform all the time – that's all – the pills are handy now and again – there's nothing new in that – it's for your benefit not mine

Tara i don't want bits of you

Peter alright we'll leave it for a while and i'll not have to take it

Tara it's not that

Peter what

Tara i don't know

Peter if you don't know why are you giving me all this fucking shit

Tara i tried to be you for a moment but it didn't work

Peter what

Tara i nearly had sex with someone else

Peter who

Tara just someone – no one

Peter do you love him

Tara what

Peter do you love him

Tara no

Peter keep it to yourself then

Tara is that how you think we should deal with this

Peter i just said

Tara this isn't like one of your clients

Peter you're still here – i'm still here – that says something

Tara i want to tell you

Peter why

Tara i don't know

Peter what then

Tara what then what

Peter tell me

Tara i was sitting having a drink – in the hotel bar you work from – looking at this man – an older man

Peter how old

Tara is that important

Peter no

Tara in his fifties

Peter that is old

Tara that's part of it – i was watching him – i sort of picked him out – randomly nearly –

i asked him did he want a drink – we talked for a while – i flirted with him and told him he could fuck me if he wanted to – we talked

Peter what do you mean – we talked

Tara we spoke to each other

Peter in a way we don't

Tara no not really

Peter not really

Tara i could talk to anybody you know – i wouldn't have to fuck them

Peter we talk

Tara it wasn't like that anyway – once i made my mind up i was going on the journey i just said what needed to be said whenever i needed to say it

Peter so you nearly fucked someone

Tara he's a good man

Peter so now i have to care about him

Tara i used him – and it didn't work – it didn't make a difference

Peter people get used

Tara shut up – shut up – eventually i talked him round to having sex – he thought it was his decision but it wasn't – he wanted to fuck outside – near a busy street – said he wanted the noise of the street around him – walking there i was excited – it felt like – living life on the edge – a bit – not mad but risky – alive – picking up someone i wouldn't normally and just fucking them – someone married – i thought it would all be different – but it wasn't – i was standing in this doorway kissing some old man – his mouth was dry – kissing some old man in a doorway that smelt of piss – it was pathetic – i thought it was going to make a difference – i thought it was going to make my life better – i was waiting on him putting his hand up my skirt but he didn't – he just kissed me again with his dry mouth – that's all he wanted

Peter i'm sorry

Tara why are you sorry

Peter it's sad when that happens

Tara that's your reaction

Peter we're mature people

Tara no we're not

Peter i choose to believe we are – there are different ways to lead your life – other people can't force you to live the way they do – i answer to no one – i don't clock in and clock out for fuck-all money – and i don't bring a fucking lunch box to work – people are like fucking sheep – told what to do all the time and they just do it – told what to think – told how to fucking feel – you live the life i've led you make up your own fucking rules

Tara what life

Peter that's my business

Tara tell me

Peter no – you want to fuck some old geezer to live life on the edge – you live life on the edge now if only you'd wake up and fucking see that – there are different types of life that are worth living – you don't always have to see the fucked-up side of things

Tara that's it is it – that's you being an adult – feeling sad for me

Peter it's me caring about you

Tara no it isn't – it's a fucking lie – you think that's the same thing as saying i love you don't you – you think that's like saying i love you so much i forgive you for hurting me – and also – by the way – i see your sadness – wanker – i didn't hurt you because you didn't feel hurt – you don't give a fuck about me – you don't love me

Tara exits.

Peter go on fuck off – i'll do what i want – i've always done what i want – tara come back – please tara come back

Tara enters.

don't leave

Tara this isn't right

Peter what can i do

Tara tell me the truth – fucking say it

Peter i need you

Tara not enough

Peter i have to earn money – i ignore what's happening to me in order to do that

Tara what's happening to you

Peter fuck off – everybody does that – i'm no different – working in tesco's – yeah very good – you know what i mean

Tara it's different

Peter different – fucking different – how the fuck can you not know that telling me you nearly fucked some old man because you were bored or fucking confused or something isn't going to hurt me

Tara because of the way we live i don't know it

Peter i fuck people for money not sport

Tara there's two lives being lived out here not one

Peter i know that

Tara do you – since you started working as a whore you haven't told me you love me

Peter if i tell you that i'm going to have to stop – and what the fuck are we going to do then – live normal shit fuckin lives – and nothing happens – how the fuck is that enough

Tara tell me you love me

Peter i was with this woman – middle-aged woman – hadn't paid for sex before – it's stupid like but there's something sweet about that – people like that need to talk – talk things through – what they're doing is painting a picture – i have to try and fit in with the picture – you need to have stories in your head – different stories – different pictures of who you are – some of them when you say them out loud you like and you think i could've been that – i could live with that – others are just shit you make up using whatever colours there are around you – some are dark and full of pain – some are light and fluffy – the way this woman was talking i knew she wanted the stories mixed up – so she could spot i was making stuff up and eventually get to the real me – it's difficult to be real and make shit up – one gets in the way of the other

Tara tell me you love me

Peter i love you

She kisses him.

Tara it'll be alright

Peter i know

The same morning. Joan and Tom have just had sex.

Joan my lip's bleeding – could you get me a hanky

He does.

Tom sorry

Joan no it's fine

Tom do you want a cup of tea or something

Joan no i'm ok

Tom right

Joan are you ok

Tom yeah sure

Joan really

Tom joan i'm fine

Joan that was different

Tom yeah

Joan different in a good way

Tom joan stop – look i'm fine – it's not – y'know – jesus – it's fine – it's cool

Joan what then

Tom i was ashamed – ashamed that i hadn't been unfaithful

Joan let's just leave it

Tom listen to me – i'm going to tell you this – you said why didn't you tell me – well i'm going to tell you – i wanted – i wanted to fuck this girl . . .

Joan girl – i thought you said she was in her mid-thirties – you said mid-thirties

Tom are you really going to go into one about this now – she was younger

Joan how young

Tom joan for christ sake – this is not a moment for you to get all fucked-up – you understand – not an opportunity for you to create a drama after the fact – the incident's over – this is the aftermath – right

Joan right – but i know you understand or you wouldn't have lied about her age

Tom are you going to let me do this

Joan yes

Tom i wanted to fuck her but couldn't

Joan you couldn't get a hard-on

Tom why do you keep using those words

Joan i don't know – i like it – i like saying the words hard-on – i'll stop though – you couldn't physically you mean

Tom no – i couldn't let myself

Joan but you wanted to

Tom of course i did

Joan there's no of course about it

Tom yes there is

Joan you could love me without question – maybe then the of course mightn't have entered your head

Tom why do i have to keep telling you that's not what it's like

Joan because i don't believe you

Tom i was looking at this person

Joan say it – young – say it

Tom i was looking at this young girl – she was looking into my face – she was asking me to be alive – to do something that would make me hear my own heartbeat – i'm a fifty-seven-year-old man that's afraid of living – i thought maybe you noticed that about me so i stood in silence hoping for a moment that you thought i was the type of man that lived life – that's a harder thing to say than whether you've fucked someone else or not – i was in work a few days before this – sitting on my own having a cup of tea – i thought to myself – throughout my life i should've fucked more women – nothing to do with a numbers thing – i don't want to be one of those men that sit on barstools and say i'm a great fella because i fucked seventeen women – i just mean i should've made connect with more people in that way – just like saying to them hello i know you're alive – hello – i don't know – what was it you said last night – if you feel it why do you assume i don't – well – is that the way you feel

Joan and if the answer's yes what should i do about it – that's not something you pretend to cure with a rubber dress and talc

Tom a decision has to be made

Joan yes

Tom are we going to leave each other

Joan no i don't think so – do you think we are

Tom no – it's too late

Joan i'm sure there's a better way of putting that tom

Tom we're too far into the journey to stop now

Joan that's it then – just this

Tom maybe

Silence.

Joan do you remember when we first started going out with each other – if you don't say you don't – it's a long time ago – you don't have to remember

Tom why would i not remember

Joan i don't know – you just mightn't – our first date you brought me to the pictures – that night – there was something – you know – something between us – we didn't set the world on fire – but you know what i mean

Tom i vaguely remember there being some tiny tiny tiny spark between us – not a flash of lightning that would blind you – but definitely a spark that might make you blink

Joan very good – the day you met me was the best day of your life

Tom that's what this is about – you telling me that

Joan no – true and all as it is – i've never told you this before

Tom why

Joan because i'd forgotten actually – at the time of our first date i was going out with another boy as well

Tom who

Joan you wouldn't know him

Tom i might – who

Joan a fella called tommy doyle

Tom squarehead doyle – he had a big head on him the size of a tv screen

Joan he didn't have a square head – lovely lookin fella he was

Tom no square head what – i played football with him a few times – useless at headers – off the corner of his head like a bullet every time – squarehead doyle – if i had've known you were going out with him there's no way we would've been at the pictures – squarehead doyle – you better not tell me you had sex with him

Joan we both know i didn't

Tom i only have your word for that – having sex with squarehead doyle is something you'd bring to the grave with you

Joan you're full of shit you know that

Tom so from squarehead to me – you moved up a right few divisions there – did he not have a turn in his eye as well

Joan don't start me

Tom and what

Joan i can't remember her name

Tom who

Joan some girl you used to go out with – what was her name

Tom don't know

Joan you do know you liar – not – no – it was m – something m – maureen – that's it – absolute scrubber

Tom lovely girl – very kind and generous

Joan a dirty scrubber from the top of her head . . .

Tom her normal shaped head

Joan if there was a school for scrubbers she would've been the headmistress

Tom there was a school for scrubbers and you went to it – never mind her anyway – squarehead – what about him

Joan after you walked me home i went round to his house – we kissed and i let him grope me – it wasn't the same though – it was less – it wasn't nothing – it was just less than it was before – that was because i had already kissed you

He kisses her.

Tom i know – do you fancy going out – we'll go out and have a drink somewhere

Joan stay here – we'll have a drink here – in bed

Tom fair enough – what do you want a gin and tonic

Joan yeah

Tom exits. Joan sits up in bed, puts lipstick on and looks at herself in a hand mirror.

Tom (*offstage*) where's the tonic

Joan beside the fridge

Tom you know what i was thinking

Joan what

Tom we haven't seen our julie for a while – i'll open up a new bottle of tonic this one's flat – we should invite julia over some night

Joan yeah sure – what about monday

Tom monday's fine

Joan be good to see her

Tom yeah be good to see her

Lights fade to dark.